PREFACE

After viewing my WALKING WITH WILDLIFE book series, I was asked to do a photography presentation for the local bird club. I am a self-taught photographer and regularly break the rules often prescribed by photographers! I experiment with shutter speed, aperture priority and manual settings to achieve different effects. Practice makes perfect ... well, that's the theory anyway.

This book summarises my presentation in which I will show you how I try to improve on the photos I take. So go out, explore with your camera and be prepared to experiment and have fun!

First Published 2025 by Jenny Dyer
For further information
contact through facebook page

Walking with Wildlife

or website

www.walkingwithwildlife.com.au

Text: © Jennifer Dyer 2025
Photography: © Jennifer Dyer 2024

All rights reserved. No part of this publication may be reproduced, stored in a retrieval system, or transmitted in any form or by any means electronic or mechanical, or by photocopying or otherwise without prior written permission of the author or copyright holder.

ISBN 978-1-7640280-2-8

Cover and Artwork: Jenny Dyer

Walking with Wildlife ™

Author and Photographer
Jenny Dyer

BOOK 9 - BIRD PHOTOGRAPHY TIPS

CROPPING IS SOMETIMES NECESSARY. Birds move around … be patient and keep focusing and clicking and don't stop clicking until you're satisfied or they've flown away. The experts never show you their not-so-good photos like this one. This photo was spoilt by the half birds on the right side which offer little to the overall image, so don't be afraid to crop the image.

This one also requires cropping to position the model better in the photo.

Sometimes insufficient zoom on your camera leaves your subject too small. This photo of the grey-crowned babbler was cropped and enhanced in my photo editing program.

Sometimes my little photography apprentice walks in front of my camera and wrecks the photo but this one of a babbler can easily be cropped.

This is another crop and enhance job for this pair of pale-headed rosellas. Using RAW files gives more data to enable brightening the image to obtain real life colours.

13

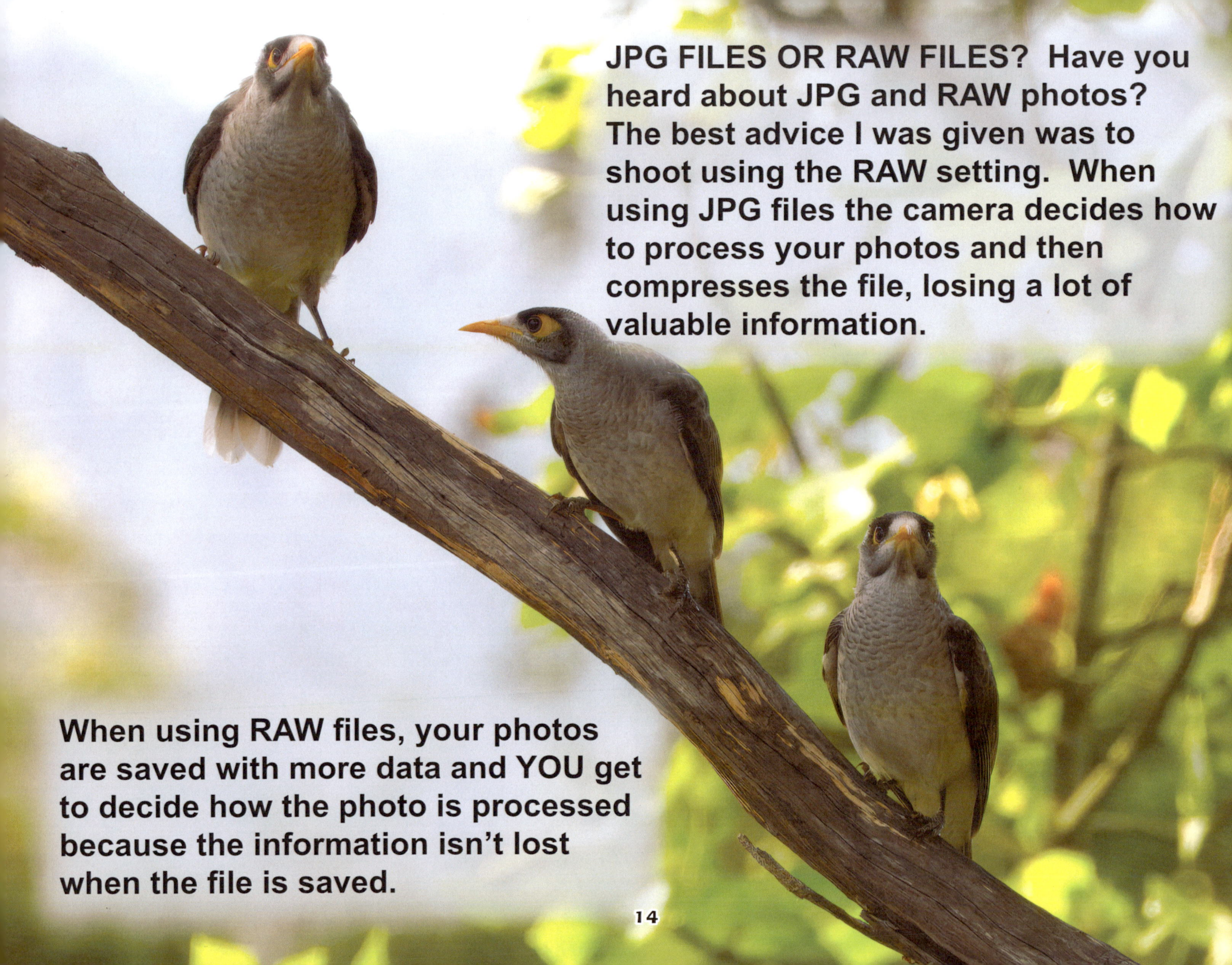

JPG FILES OR RAW FILES? Have you heard about JPG and RAW photos? The best advice I was given was to shoot using the RAW setting. When using JPG files the camera decides how to process your photos and then compresses the file, losing a lot of valuable information.

When using RAW files, your photos are saved with more data and YOU get to decide how the photo is processed because the information isn't lost when the file is saved.

This is the photo after I processed the file. Using curves, shadows, exposure, contrast and brightness in a software program I have enhanced this image. This is a very time-consuming process.

RAW or JPG?   You can still get very good photos using JPG files, so the choice is yours. These two photos were taken using JPG format. Working with RAW files takes more time and memory on your computer but can give much better results in difficult lighting situations.

GOLDEN HOUR. The red-backed fairy wrens on these two pages were taken with the lighting coming from behind me in the late afternoon, just before sunset and in the early morning, just after sunrise. This is often referred to as "the golden hour" and is the ideal time to photograph. JPG works well in this ideal lighting.

GOLDEN HOUR. The beautiful early morning light was ideal to portray this red-backed fairy wren at her best.

The morning sun also lit up the feathers of this female king parrot.

The late afternoon light enhanced this pheasant coucal's feathers and the eyes came alive.

These two photos were taken in the middle of the day when the light is supposed to be too harsh for photography.

It doesn't hurt to bend the rules occasionally because it allowed for a very fast shutter speed to freeze the water droplets.

BACKLIGHTING WORKS. Both these photos are backlit with the exposure increased by 2 stops. The light shining through the feathers of the pheasant coucal highlights their beautiful pattern.

Backlighting outlines this male red-backed fairy wren's body and the branches.

Breaking the rules about shooting into the sun can give an interesting effect.

Cloud cover gives even lighting with no harsh shadows.

WATCHING THE LIGHT. These two photos were taken in the same place but the sun cast dreadful shadows over the lizard in this photo.

The sun went behind the cloud for just a few seconds and made this photo possible, once again emphasising the importance of watching the lighting. With practice you will get to read the light.

Look at that glint in his eye!

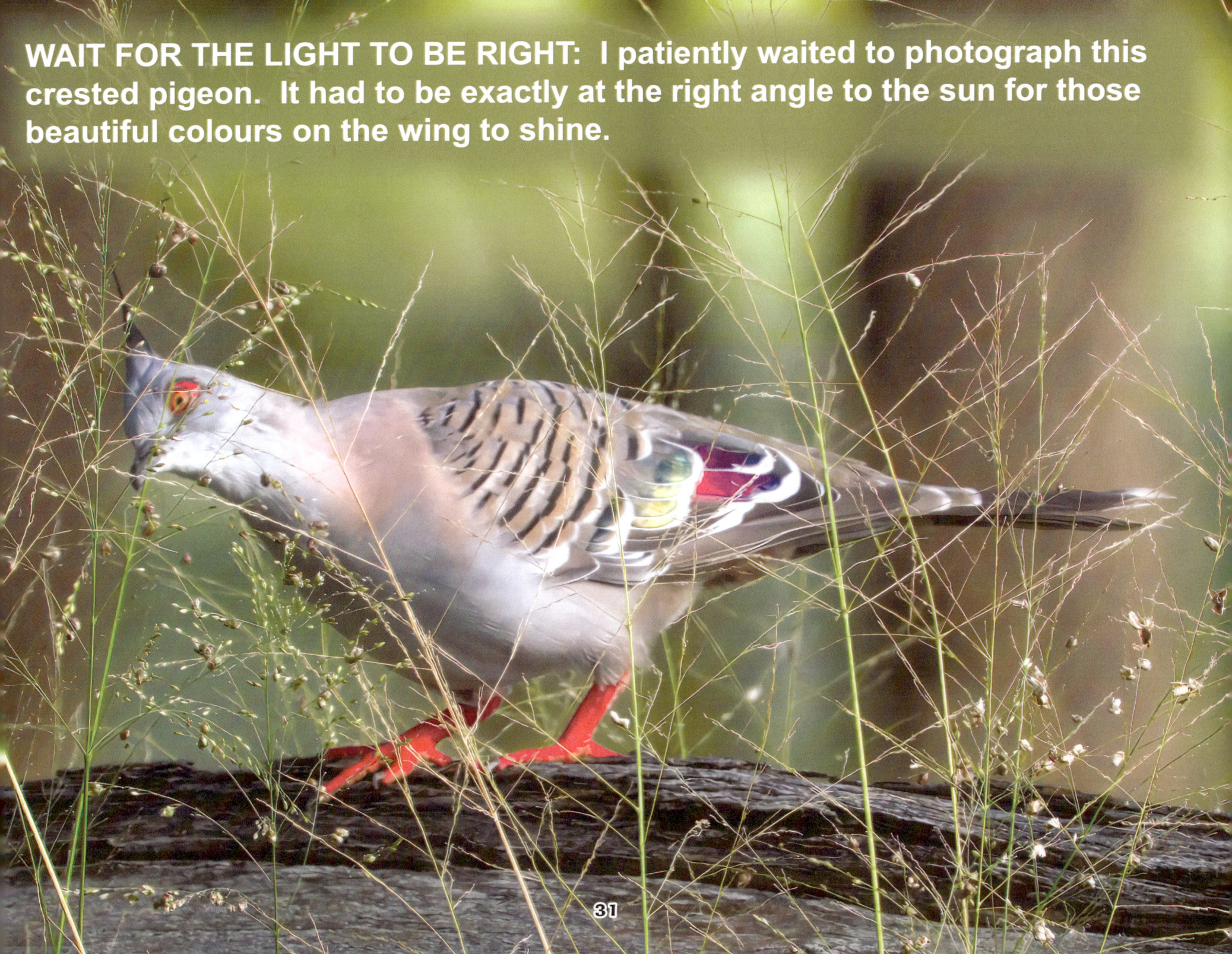

WAIT FOR THE LIGHT TO BE RIGHT: I patiently waited to photograph this crested pigeon. It had to be exactly at the right angle to the sun for those beautiful colours on the wing to shine.

CHANGING YOUR LOCATION. These two photos were taken a minute apart. This one was taken into the rising sun allowing me to create this striking silhouette.

I moved 20 metres further to the south east so I didn't have the bright sky behind the brown falcon.

Two entirely different photos of the same bird within a minute. I creatively adjusted the lighting on the first photo.

When I came across this black kite in the early morning, I was in the bottom of a big gully, looking into the bright sky in the east. I adjusted the settings so the bird would be exposed properly, but that meant the sky was blown out ie over-exposed. I have a rule for myself "always take a photo before you move" as the bird may be frightened by movement and fly away.

I moved about 8 metres to the north up the other side of the gully, putting the mountain behind my subject allowing for a perfectly exposed photo. I also zoomed in on the bird as it was now concealed behind branches. Which shot do you think is the better?

The GLINT IN THE EYE makes the subject come alive. What do you reckon? Same place but just a slight turn of the head by this restless flycatcher makes a world of difference. (They turn their heads frequently.)

The same pheasant coucal, with similar poses, illustrates the importance of eye contact. Which photo do you think creates more impact?

Once again, just a slight difference in these two photos of a kookaburra. It's all in the eye contact or the little glint that makes one photo more alive than the other.

I also moved just a fraction to the left to try and improve the lighting and get the branch away from his beak. You can never be too picky.

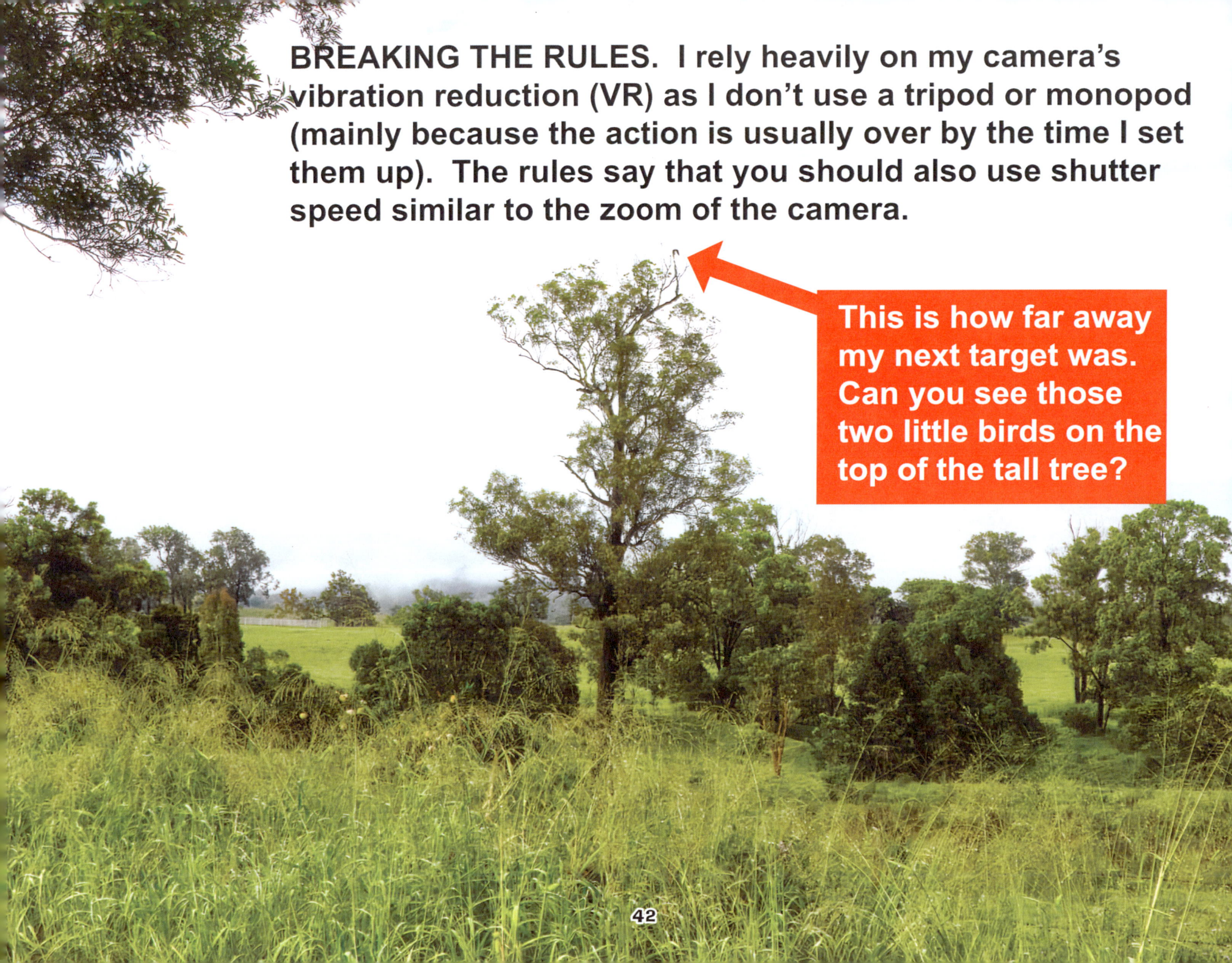

BREAKING THE RULES. I rely heavily on my camera's vibration reduction (VR) as I don't use a tripod or monopod (mainly because the action is usually over by the time I set them up). The rules say that you should also use shutter speed similar to the zoom of the camera.

This is how far away my next target was. Can you see those two little birds on the top of the tall tree?

Channel-billed Cuckoos.

I used aperture priority to set the F stop to F8 (so I can have the largest depth of field for my camera). The ISO was set on 100 (which gives better detail).

The shutter speed automatically set to 1/180 second. I think the VR of the camera works well at low shutter speed.

The zoom was 2400mm.

LOOK FOR A BIT OF ACTION. These birds were on a feeding frenzy so I stayed and took heaps of photos. This one only has a slight glint in the eye but has the added bonus of a grub in her mouth.

That stick insect disappeared in a second …. Two quick gulps and it was completely gone. I had to focus quickly as these birds were flitting all over the place searching for a feed.

BIRDS IN FLIGHT. This magpie goose was photographed in shutter priority with the speed set fairly high. This photo, although a clear action shot, was just too busy to use in my book so I …. Well, can you guess what I did!

Sometimes when there's action about (and there isn't enough light) I use manual mode to underexpose the photo. It captures more details and freezes the action. I use a fast shutter speed/low ISO/large F stop in this case.

These image were "almost" black before enhancing it in my photo editing program.

So let's get CREATIVE!

51

www.ingramcontent.com/pod-product-compliance
Lightning Source LLC
Chambersburg PA
CBRC101355070526
44583CB00010B/196